Beyon Spirituality

Victimhood and Christian Hope

David Kettle

Co-ordinator of the Gospel and Our Culture Network

GROVE BOOKS LIMITED
RIDLEY HALL RD CAMBRIDGE CB3 9HU

Contents

1   Introduction 3

2   Assessing a Culture of Tragic Spirituality 5

3   Naming the Demon: What is a 'Tragic Sense of Life'? 13

4   A Tragic Sense of Life and the Hope of the Gospel 18

5   When the Gospel Itself Becomes Captive to Evasion 24

6   Bibliography 28

First Impression November 2005
ISSN 0262-799X
ISBN 1 85174 607 2

Introduction

Victimhood harrows the human soul.

Whether we are victims ourselves, or witness others as victims, the experience can plunge our lives into darkness. Victimhood, whether inflicted by another or by misfortune, has power to overwhelm us and this power can be seen at work in the public imagination of Western culture today.

This booklet is about the light of Christ shining into the darkness of tragedy and victimhood. In it we shall explore how God, through the crucified and risen Jesus Christ, releases us from the spell under which these things can hold us. Let us therefore ask Christ for grace to face what presents itself as unfaceable as we now explore victimhood and cultural responses to it today, and bring these into the light of Christ.

Let us think of a victim—a real one. A Bosnian woman, it is reported, was given back her baby by soldiers to suckle at her breast. She was, however, the object of awful mockery; the baby's head had no body.

> *This booklet is about the light of Christ shining into the darkness of tragedy and victimhood*

The thought of such a thing sears our souls. We want to believe this has not happened, that it could not possibly happen; but it *has*. We want to *do* something, or to *undo* something—but we are *powerless*. As witnesses in imagination of this event we are drawn with the victim herself into a profound spiritual trial, or test—can we live open to this reality, and remain open to the reality of a good God? Can faith, hope and love remain alive in us when they are so brutally mocked?

Jesus taught his disciples to ask to be spared the trial or testing of their faith in a good and trustworthy God. This is the meaning of 'Do not lead us into temptation.' In popular imagination 'temptation' is about the impulse to act against God's good direction, like Adam and Eve in the garden of Eden. And to be sure, this is a temptation to doubt God's trustworthiness. So too, however, is the impulse either to turn away or despair when trust in a good Father is taunted intolerably by tragedy and victimhood. In another garden—the garden of Gethsemane—Jesus prayed that he might not drink the cup of such trial, and warned his closest disciples to pray similarly to be spared the ultimate test of their faith.

Throughout his public ministry, Jesus had reached out to victims of one kind or another, freeing them from the trial of victimhood. These were practical signs of God's kingdom at hand. When Jesus then embraced extreme victimhood himself, he did so daring to believe that through it God would open the way decisively for the coming of this kingdom.

Seen in this setting, it may appear that the keen sensibility towards victims which marks Western culture today is Christian. It may seem appropriate for Christians wholeheartedly to endorse this sensibility, and to draw from it guidance and energy for their Christian life and witness today.

> *The gospel liberates us with unquenchable hope, dignity and forbearance*

However, the gospel calls us decisively beyond this. It indeed addresses the same spectres which inflame this cultural sensibility, but does so in a more radical way. In so doing, it breaks their spiritual bondage over us, liberating us to live with unquenchable hope, dignity and forbearance. Below we shall explore this act of God's grace through the gospel.

In chapter two of this booklet I will appraise the keen sensibility towards victims which marks our culture, setting this in the context of Christ's own engagement with victimhood. I will focus especially upon what I shall call 'tragic' spirituality and the distinctive way in which tragic victims evoke a sense of the sacred. We shall consider several evaluations of this spirituality, before concluding that it expresses a 'tragic sense of life.'

This sense of life constitutes nothing less than a worldview which contradicts the hope of the gospel. In chapter three I will explore this as an evasion of faith riddled, for all its sense of compulsion, with self-deception and contradiction. In chapter four I shall uncover how this is addressed with trust and hope in the Bible, and above all in Jesus Christ who draws us into his own ultimate victimhood, vindication and liberation by God.

But Christ-inspired trust and hope always remain vulnerable in the world to hijack by the evasion from which the gospel has released us. In chapter five I shall illustrate the risk of disempowerment of the gospel even among Christians themselves and in their very conception of Christ. Finally I will summarize the Christian vocation to a self-aware spirituality of imaginative, practical, Christ-like engagement with victimhood today.

Assessing a Culture of Tragic Spirituality

2

How does tragic victimhood shape our thinking and feeling in Western culture today?

What is its spiritual significance for the health of our own souls, and in the context of Christian mission?

Victimhood as the Occasion of Spiritual Encounter

'Religious' expressions of feeling towards tragic victims have increased noticeably in Western culture recently. When the Princess of Wales died in 1997, people placed lighted candles, flowers and other memorials in huge numbers throughout Britain. In 2002, the murder of two young schoolgirls provoked a flood of gestures. Visitors lit over 15,000 candles in Soham Parish Church, wrote a similar number of letters, laid similar quantities of flowers in the churchyard and gave around 2,000 teddy bears. Often today, roadside floral tributes are laid at the scene of traffic accidents which are sometimes tended like graves. Formal acts of memorial for victims are held in the public arenas of politics, education and mass media programming. In 2005, with substantial government funding, public remembrance of the victims of Auschwitz took place on the 60th anniversary of its liberation. In 2007 there will be public recollection of the victims of the dehumanizing slave trade on the 200th anniversary of the Abolition of the Slave Trade Act. The marking of tragedy has, of course, long been part of English church life in its funeral ministry, and since World War One in its Remembrance Sunday services. Recently, however, the religious expression in public of feeling over tragic victims has grown in prominence and has taken new forms.

> *The religious expression in public of feeling over tragic victims has grown in prominence, and has taken new forms*

Feeling towards victims also shows itself in our culture in militant posturing on behalf of victims and groups liable to victimization. Abortion practitioners get murdered, animal vivisectionists fire-bombed. The philosophy which inspired the Muslim Brotherhood and Osama Bin Laden burns with a sense of the victimhood of Muslims at the hands of Jews and Christians; the author

Sayid Qut'b was himself a long-standing political prisoner finally executed. Such outrage over victims may not seem at first sight itself a spiritual or religious matter. Behind it, however, lie feelings of the sort people have when what they count sacred is violated. There is a kind of exaltation of the (profaned) rights of victims which endows these victims (when their rights have been profaned) with sacred status. Indeed, sacred status can be acquired by entire groups of people in this way as 'belonging to a certain group' gets identified with 'being a victim.' Thus, to be a woman, or Jewish, or black-skinned may identify a person, for some, with *an object of desecration* in the form of sexism, anti-semitism or racism. Other groups acquire similar status when seen as victims of 'phobias.' As a result, according to René Girard, victim power has today established a 'permanent inquisition' within an ideology which 'takes over and "radicalizes" the concern for victims in order to paganize it' (2001, p 178, 180). In the US, Os Guinness can write of 'a hierarchy of group privileges and sensitivities that are ranked according to their cultural standing in victimhood (a sort of "more victimized than thou")' in which rights—that is, sacred entitlements—run riot (1992, p 90). In Britain, fear of litigation—fear, at root, of facing the absolute claims upon oneself of a victim—has grown to the point of undermining the fabric of mutual trust within community life. It is bringing erosions of freedom which, a few decades ago, few apart from George Orwell would have conceived.

In Britain, fear of facing the absolute claims upon oneself of a victim has grown to the point of undermining trust

Women's Institutes are becoming afraid to sell home baking, and schools are weighing up whether to chop down their trees for fear that children will eat their berries or slip on their fallen leaves. The intimidation felt here in the West is a distant echo of that felt by citizens under the huge indefinable scope of legislation in Stalin's Russia.

The 'Western guilt complex' is another factor in this state of affairs. This complex can be so paralysing that, as the journalist and self-avowed atheist Anthony Browne has pointed out, even though Christians around the world are the largest single group on earth victimized for their religion, the West consistently glosses their plight because it thinks of them (as often do their persecutors) as 'white'—as Western transplants and accomplices in Western imperialism. In such ways, modern victim sensibility can ironically sponsor or collude with new forms of victimization.

A sense of the sacred, then, animates both gestures towards tragic victims and gestures of militancy in support of victims actual and potential. Despite differences between them, both kinds of gestures are fuelled fundamentally by the same spirit, as we shall see. But it is grief that lies more deeply than militancy at the heart of this spirit. I shall therefore dwell mainly on this and the 'tragic' spirituality associated with it.

Our culture invites us to embrace 'tragic' spirituality. The vital question is, how should we respond to this in the light of Christ? Most certainly the Christ of the gospels calls us to reach out with God's love to victims of tragedy and oppression and to those who grieve over them. Equally he would have us work tire-lessly and patiently to prevent tragedies and acts of injustice or victimization in the first place. The Christian imperative in these matters can hardly be overstated. But does this mean we should join in strident rheto-ric on behalf of victims? And when faced with victims beyond restoration, should we align ourselves with those animated by tragic spirituality?

When faced with victims beyond restoration, should we align ourselves with those animated by tragic spirituality?

Tragic spirituality and victim sensibility press for evaluation in the light of Christ today. Among possible appraisals, I shall discuss three.

Should We Defer to Tragic Spirituality?

We might say something like the following:

> What we find here is a sense of the sacred which, as anthropologists tell us, appears in its own form in every culture. In tragic spirituality it takes a form not recognizably Christian, because our culture is no longer much informed by Christian faith. Traditional religion no longer connects with the religious instinct which finds expression here. The church must draw alongside people, affirm their religious instinct, and learn from them how to connect with it.

Grace Davie suggests that even in a secularist society, a sense of sacred may surface when 'normal' ways of living are, for one reason or another, suspended and 'something far more instinctive comes to the fore.' Tragedy is one such occasion.

Should Christians therefore affirm tragic spirituality? Certainly in the past, when materialism seemed the great enemy of faith and any sense of the sacred or spiritual was informed by a Christian cultural heritage, a sense of the sacred or spiritual commended itself. Today, however, our very understanding of 'spirituality' and 'the sacred' are no longer shaped by Christian faith, but by phenomena standing in quite ambiguous relation to Christian faith.

But, more deeply, Christian faith has never stood simply for belief that 'sacredness is to be found in the world,' although many sociologists and anthropologists seem to think so. In actual fact Christianity strips nature and culture of any intrinsic sacred status endowed upon it. It continues to do so even in secularist culture today, which (despite its self-understanding) has its own sacred taboos. Long ago, biblical faith 'de-sacralized' the sacred world of Baalism, turning Canaanite sacred fertility rites into celebrations of God's sovereign and saving acts in history. Such acts found their consummation in Jesus Christ, in whom all creation is made new, and in whom the truly sacred is found. In him, the entire material, secular (that is, provisional) world is to be transformed into the kingdom of God.

> *In him, the entire material, secular world is to be transformed into the kingdom of God*

In summary, we need to be discerning towards any contemporary sense of 'the sacred,' including that of tragic spirituality. We must reject beliefs and practices which posit an inherently sacred world, finding the truly sacred rather in Christ who transforms secular life throughout.

Should We Scorn Tragic Spirituality?

Should we rather scorn public expressions of grief today as fake? In *Conspicuous Compassion* (2004), Patrick West writes 'We live in a post-emotional age, one characterized by crocodile tears and manufactured emotion.' He sees extravagant public displays of grief for people one has never met as 'recreational' grief, 'undertaken as an enjoyable event, much like going to a football match or the last night at the proms.' He dubs this 'mourning sickness.' The phoney character of these displays leads, according to West, to 'compassion inflation.' Recalling the practice of keeping a two-minute silence on Remembrance Day, he writes:

> When a group called Hedgeline calls for a two-minute silence to remember all the 'victims' whose neighbours have grown towering hedges, we truly have reached the stage where this gesture has been emptied of meaning.

Patrick West appeals to the theories of Stjepan Meštrovic's book *Postemotional Society*. Meštrovic claims that not only our thinking but also our feelings are widely manufactured in mass society today. The modern rationalization of life has extended beyond thinking to feeling, in a kind of 'McDonaldization of emotions.' Bite-size, pre-packaged emotions such as vicarious indignation are manufactured and cued in new acts of mass manipulation. Emotions have not disappeared, but they have become widely distorted into synthetic, quasi-emotions severed from thought and yielding no action.

The journalist Madeleine Bunting takes issue with West. She notes that Right-Wing Think Tanks (*Conspicuous Compassion* was published by *Civitas*) have a habit of claiming that people today bleat about things endured by previous generations without fuss. But there really is an escalating weight of emotional distress abroad, she believes, and it comes precisely from the disorienting experience of rapid and apparently senseless change driven by market capitalism in recent decades—it is an inevitable consequence of its policies. Seen in this setting, it is largely beside the point that emotional distress is articulated in neurotic or 'fake' ways; the distress is real.

In brief, then, we may judge that behind gestures of compassion, rituals of powerlessness and militant postures alike with all the ambiguities there lies real pain. Melvyn Matthews has written:

> It is the pain, the actual deadening, horrifying pain of living in the modern which is at the heart of things. Most of us totally underestimate the existence and importance of this pain as a factor in our lives. It is glossed consistently. But the pain forces us to disown responsibility ...The existence of this pain deadens and numbs our moral existence. Our reserves of compassion seep away, our desire for real living is undermined by the task of moving from one day to another with the minimum of disaster. (1987, p 99)

Although Patrick West finds in 'conspicuous compassion' only a pretence of caring about and helping victims, this may reflect a sense precisely that what begs to be done *cannot* be done. 'Spiritual' gestures such as lighting candles are not to be scorned as fake, but seen as (futile) gestures of overwhelming felt powerlessness. Here, I believe, we come to the heart of tragic spirituality and to its distinctive 'sense of the sacred.'

Should We See Here a Returning 'Tragic Sense of Life' Devoid of Christian Hope?

The word 'tragic' gets applied loosely to many misfortunes, but it also has more intense meaning when it refers, for example, to a 'tragic figure.' Here it connotes a certain *tragic sense of life*. This is ignited typically by a dramatic encounter in which life and its deeply-held value are mocked by catastrophic violation without remedy or compensation. This encounter is then taken as spelling the fundamental truth of human life: as human beings we inhabit an alien and malign world which will have the last word upon us. We are victims in a correspondingly radical sense. When we are seized by a tragic sense of life, we take into the heart of ourselves this denial or contradiction of our ourselves and our humanity as radically victimized.

In *The Death of Tragedy* (1961), George Steiner traced the decline of the tragic sense of life as expressed in drama since classical Greek Tragedy. He saw this decline as reflecting the influence of Jewish and Christian belief in a good God who will finally see justice done. More recently, however, researchers have asked whether there is not a return in our culture of a tragic sense of life. David Hay and Kate Hunt, in their report *Understanding the Spirituality of People Who Don't go to Church*, write:

> We are wondering whether, forty years on from Steiner's analysis, after Auschwitz and after the many other atrocities of the 20th century, we see in post-Christian society the return of a tragic sense of life...If at the deepest level there is a conviction that life at depth is pitiless and utterly meaningless, then the optimism of Christianity becomes incredible. The people we spoke to were well aware of this, and it is an issue that church people need to face much more directly in their dialogue with secular culture. (2000, p 38)

Here we are led to a third possible appraisal of tragic spirituality, as embodying a returning tragic sense of life.

Is this what finds expression in public outpourings of emotion today? Contemporary gestures towards victims provide some evidence of this. The gestures over the death of the Princess of Wales were over a tragedy claiming the last word upon one already seen as a tragic victim. Roadside floral tributes at the scene of accidents, lying in sharp disjunction from their bleak public setting, speak of tragic violence done to a 'private' life; unlike the traditional grave clustered among others around the building where a faithful God is worshipped, such tokens grant violation the last word. Gifts of teddy bears in memory of a lost child are so evidently enactments of futile giving and speak of unresolved feelings of powerlessness in the face of tragedy.

Gifts of teddy bears in memory of a lost child speak of unresolved feelings of powerlessness in the face of tragedy

Evidence for a returning tragic sense of life goes beyond such expressions of 'tragic spirituality' and gestures of outrage at victimhood. Loss of hope today leaves people needy, credulous and promiscuous—facts exploited (and arguably reinforced) by those who market novel therapies, goods and services. It also fuels escapism through drugs, alcohol and gambling, and through a diet of sentiment. From *The Wizard of Oz* to *The Matrix* trilogy, Hollywood intimates an unattainable salvation to the needy soul—the victorious power of positive thinking, and of self-originating choice in the face of bleak determinism. Above all, loss of hope fosters narcissism, as people turn away from the world in despair and construct a 'self' which becomes the focus of their lives. The demands of the real world and of real other people, intractable before this self, are now experienced as oppressive. Christopher Lasch has written perceptively on the 'Culture of Narcissism.' We have every reason to recognize, in our culture, the return of a tragic sense of life.

How Has it Come to This?

Why might a tragic sense of life be returning in our culture? One explanation is the disorienting social change in recent decades to which Madeleine Bunting refers, driven pitilessly by intensifying market capitalism. Writing from the US, Edward Farley describes this social change:

> The predominantly marketing and consumer society in which most Westerners live has transformed virtually all traditional institutions (governments, corporations, universities) and created new or transformed institutions (the media, entertainment and leisure, professional sports, communications)…Moreover, the social shift I describe has isolated certain powerful institutions (corporate, military, governmental, media, entertainment) from the influence of the co-called normative institutions such as education, religion and the arts. Indeed, the great cultural transformation of our time has changed the character of these normative institutions, drawing them into the marketplace and the world of image-making, of salesmanship and of managerial orientations. This massive shift has had a devastating effect on the once-deep cultural values that exerted their force upon most of society's institutions—values of truth, duty, discipline, reading, beauty, family, tradition, justice among many others.

In the deeper background lie those huge conflicts which ravaged Europe and so much of the world in the course of the 20th century. These were such that in 1983 Alexander Solzhenitsyn could say 'Today's world has reached a stage that, if it had been described to preceding centuries, would have called forth the cry "This is the apocalypse!"' These conflicts undermined modern confidence in progress towards a better world, destroying its underlying faith in human goodness and rationality. No amount of rhetoric by today's politicians

These conflicts undermined modern confidence in progress towards a better world

about modernization, or by businessmen about wealth-creation, can replace that exalted vision or the altruism it inspired to serve the public good. Instead we have a widely felt legacy of guilt over Western exploitation of peoples and resources, an uneasy conscience about the West's current global economic and military hegemony, and apprehension over future prospects for our planet.

At a more personal level, individuals today find themselves disoriented by lack of participation in a morally cohesive community following changes in lifestyle and values in the 1960s. These changes have brought in their wake widespread insecurity for children in their upbringing, and a decline in job security arising from new employment practices. These and other socially generated insecurities have tended to erode people's sense of personal worth and hope.

The personal disorientation resulting from all this is dramatically portrayed by the Australian poet Michael Leunig:

> Something is amiss. It's like when birds suddenly can't find their flight to Alaska. We are in a particular time in history when it's immensely stressful to be alive. I would say we are in the midst of pillaging and rape of the psychological eco-system, the ecology of the soul. There's a great, delicate, interconnected ecology that goes on in people's lives. We are defiling it, exploiting it, and this will have tremendous consequences for the emotional health of society.

Meanwhile, for a century or more, Christian spiritual resources have been depleting. Christian faith and hope are less readily to hand for the power to live with the change, conflict and insecurity of our age.

All of these things have allowed another spirit to gain ascendancy.

Questions for Discussion

1 'In Christian history they see nothing but persecutions, acts of oppression, inquisitions…a pale imitation of the authentic crusade against oppression and persecution for which they would carry the banner themselves…' (Rene Girard, p 180-1). The author attributes this to the Antichrist. Discuss.

2 'I have often been asked "What is the greatest difficulty you face in moving from India to England?" I have always answered: "The disappearance of hope" (Lesslie Newbigin, 1983, p 1). Discuss.

3 'Those people crying loudest for retribution so often seem to be the least affected' (Andrew Rice, whose brother David was killed in the World Trade Centre on 9/11. Why should this be? Discuss.

Naming the Demon: What is a 'Tragic Sense of Life'? 3

How does the gift of the gospel address a tragic sense of life, a 'tragic' worldview?

In order to answer this, we must first explore further this worldview in the light of faith, and recognize what it does to our souls.

According to Christian faith, human beings are made by a good God in the image of himself and are deeply precious to him. However, the image of God is marred in us by our sin. We regularly betray God's goodness; we regularly betray each other's worth, contradicting God's image in each other and, by acting in this way, in ourselves. We are tempted to such betrayal when we are faced with heart-rending tragedy and victimhood beyond reparation—either that of someone else or our own. Here, only in the most costly, heartfelt questioning can we hold on to the reality of God's goodness and of human worth at the same time as facing the pain of their outright contradiction.

At the heart of our encounter with tragic victimhood lies this stark dissonance. We are presented on the one hand with a person of unqualified worth; on the other, with an occurrence which overtakes that person as if they were neither there nor of worth. This dissonance inflames within us huge moral and spiritual pain. It is important to recognize the moral and spiritual character of this pain. This is not just dismay over physical suffering and loss, but moral grief over what ought never to happen —an appalling violation of the imperative of goodness, a huge offence to what is right. And our pain has spiritual depth; mocked here is the very existence of the meaning and hope which tacitly grounds all moral human life.

Mocked here is the very existence of the meaning and hope which tacitly grounds all moral human life

The demands made by tragic victimhood upon us are enormous, and we are tempted strongly to evade them—betraying both God and ourselves. Such evasion may follow two directions.

Firstly, we may treat victims *dismissively*, denying the challenge their victimhood presents to us and to faith. We may simply look the other way. Or we may play down their oppression. Or we may see victims as 'different' from us, and refuse to put ourselves in their place. Or we may tell ourselves their plight must be accepted as inevitable. Or we may tell ourselves they have only themselves to blame. In each case we find reason unreasonably to dismiss demands made upon us personally, morally and spiritually to grieve over victimhood.

The tendency to dismiss victims is well recognized in society, and when identified meets with censure. Such censure has been a feature especially of modern societies in which, from time to time, the customary dismissal of one victim group or another gets acknowledged and addressed for what it is. Especially today in Western society, feeling runs high over the dismissal of various victim groups: women, racial minorities, the handicapped.

Faced with outrageous mockery of human worth and God's goodness, we may be crushed in spirit

Secondly (and this is less well recognized as evasion), we may evade the demands of victimhood upon us and upon faith by submitting to its power personally to *overwhelm and defeat* us. Faced with outrageous mockery of human worth and God's goodness, we may be crushed in spirit. We see injustice, humiliation and contempt as forever mocking us with impunity. Mockery acquires for us here ultimate status—we count it as having the last word, beyond all remedy, on humanity and God. The anguish of such inner, personal defeat defines a tragic sense of life.

When the demands of victimhood overwhelm us in this way, we may adopt a variety of stances. We may take the bad into ourselves as somehow 'deserved'; children who have been routinely abused sexually think they are to blame. We may be paralysed by self-pity in a contradictory mix of resignation and resentment. Alternatively, we may project the bad outwards. Driven by rage, we may hit out randomly at the world which has betrayed us. Prisons contain many criminals who insist that they have been framed by the world. Or we may focus implacably on certain targets which cry out for 'divine' retribution—by actions ranging from suing to suicide bombing. Or again, we may seek to compensate personally for being overwhelmed and feeling utterly in the power of 'someone' beyond ourselves, by seeking to overwhelm others in turn, and feeding upon their victim-perception of *us* as holding all power over *them*.

Importantly, such inner defeat involves positing tacitly an alien 'other.' Faced with a victim of misfortune, typically we feel with passion that the world should be such that the presence and worth of this person was upheld, where it was not. 'Somebody' should have affirmed and helped them in the same way we would have done were we able, and 'they' have *chosen* (odd as it is for us to ascribe choice in this way to 'nobody') to be absent. Faced with one who is the victim not of misfortune but of another human being, our sense that somebody should have been present to uphold the presence and worth of the victim is confronted agonisingly by the fact that somebody *was* there and *made* them their victim. Paradoxically the mockingly 'absent' agent of victimhood is all the more starkly present and active. This 'presence' of the 'absent' agent mocks the victim as correspondingly made 'absent' precisely through their 'presence as a victim' to the agent.

Simone Weil describes the 'affliction' of victimhood in terms relevant to this account, although her interpretation of such affliction differs significantly (1951, pp 66–69). She describes affliction as 'anonymous before all things; it deprives its victims of their personality and makes them into things. It is indifferent; and it is the coldness of this indifference—a metallic coldness—that freezes all those it touches right to the depths of their souls.' She notes how oppression is turned inwards here so that affliction 'stamps the soul to its very depths with the scorn, the disgust and even the self-hatred and sense of guilt and defilement which crime…should produce.' And she records the victim's complicity in all this: 'In anyone who has suffered affliction for a long enough time there is a complicity with regard to his own affliction…it is as if affliction has established itself in him like a parasite and were directing him to suit its own purposes.'

When we are overwhelmed by tragic victimhood (either our own or that of another person), we grant cosmic status to this denial of human worth and God's goodness. We count it a contradiction lying forever beyond resolution. We also allow it to penetrate and define our very selves; we 'assent' to our negation, coming under its spell. We treat ourselves as deserving 'the undeserved,' and become our own victim. This finds stark expression in the growth of self-harm such as that admitted by Olympic gold medallist Kelly Holmes. Sebastian Moore has probed self-victimization in his book *The Crucified Is No Stranger*. There is also a sense in which we become spectators of our own victimhood: transfixed, we at once distance ourselves in pity from, and identify in self-pity with, the 'other' self before us. We want to be a paralysing spectacle. In a sketch performed by Theatre Roundabout, a self-pitying woman contemplates 'the glamour of the gas oven.' It has been said that within every person who contemplates suicide there is at once a victim, an agent and an onlooker; perhaps the same can be said generally of a person who is overwhelmed by a tragic sense of life. Here lies the deepest, darkest, most unfaceable part of inner defeat by victimhood: our own hidden compliance. We ourselves assent

Transfixed, we at once distance ourselves in pity from, and identify in self-pity with, the 'other' self before us

We ourselves assent to being absent as responsible actors — absent to God, to others and to ourselves

to being absent as responsible actors—absent to God, to others and to ourselves.

Among the contradictions inherent in such a posture of inner defeat is our hidden construction of this as an experience of passive violation. We experience something taken from us or done to us as a person, and yet this way of experiencing things is shaped precisely by our evasion of the demands of faith. We construct our world in terms of ultimate violation and loss. Again, while we see ourselves as fully open to our circumstances, and indeed as paying a heavy price personally for such openness, in truth by adopting a posture of defeat we foreclose the question posed by tragic victimhood by counting it forever beyond resolution. We claim tacitly to know that the last word on human life is its denial—a spectre forever beyond facing or escaping. By making this claim, however, we evade the demands of living with the unresolved questions posed by, and remaining open to further costly engagement with, the truth of God and of human worth.

We 'consent,' then, to the paralysis of our hope here in how we interpret the world—although we conceal this from ourselves. This is the spiritual power of victimhood binding us. Empowerment to overcome this bondage is as much part of liberation for victims as is release from physical oppression.

Christian tradition has in general shown insufficient understanding of such inner personal defeat by victimhood. Two factors seem to have contributed to this:

1   There has been a tendency traditionally to think of sin as driven by pride and a spirit of rebellion and false autonomy. This has led us to see sin more readily in the oppressor than in the oppressed, and in the dismissal of victims rather than in being overwhelmed by victimhood. But the need to take seriously the sinfulness of inner personal defeat has been argued recently by Alister McFadyen who proposes, in *Bound to Sin,* that 'self-loss' is a sin—the sin of sloth. Further light is shed when we recall how the 'deadly sins' including sloth were first understood. Simon Tugwell traces them to the teachings of the Desert Fathers for whom they represented *logismoi*—trains of thought which shape how the world is seen and which have an inner momentum of their own towards deepening, enslaving perversity.

2   There has been a tendency traditionally to understand too narrowly the burden of victimhood as the pain—physical and emotional—of

bodily suffering, without acknowledging the moral and spiritual distress involved. By contrast, the South African Truth and Reconciliation Commission grasped the importance of acknowledging the truth of victimization and the responsibility of its perpetrators quite apart from issues of reparation or, for that matter, vengeance. Perhaps past neglect of such things has been the result of an emphasis on innate human sinfulness (which can mute the appeal against injustice) and on the need to embrace suffering in union with Christ.

I began by noting the rise of tragic spirituality and victim sensibility in our culture, and discerned within these a returning tragic sense of life. This 'tragic' worldview is to be understood, I have suggested, as an evasion of faith where its demands are great. We betray our faith when we are *overwhelmed and defeated* in spirit, just as much as when we *dismiss* its demands upon us. But this has not been widely recognized, for the reasons given.

Questions for Discussion

1 'Remaining [consumed by anger and hatred] locks you in a state of victimhood, making you almost dependent on the perpetrator. If you can find it in yourself to forgive then you are no longer chained to the perpetrator.' (Archbishop Desmond Tutu). Do you agree? (For the full text of his remarks, see http://www.theforgivenessproject.com/stories/desmond-tutu)

2 Share any stories of 'whistleblowers' familiar to you. Discuss the sources of the distress, and the spiritual nature of the distress, which whistleblowers often feel.

3 Gemma McCartney said after her brother's murder in Belfast: 'Only now I'm in this situation do I realise how essential justice is. You see people on TV saying they're fighting for justice and you think, why don't they just accept things and get on with the grieving process? It's only now that I realise how important justice is. Otherwise he would have died in vain.' Discuss her viewpoint.

4 Discuss the following quotation from Simone Weil's article 'The Love of God and Affliction':

   If Job cries out that he is innocent in such despairing accents, it is because he himself is beginning not to believe in it…he implores God himself to bear witness, because he no longer hears the testimony of his own conscience.' (pp 66-67)

4

A Tragic Sense of Life and the Hope of the Gospel

Starting implicitly from Christian faith, we have analysed the worldview belonging to a tragic sense of life.

Let us now consider briefly how this analysis is illustrated explicitly by, and also sheds light upon, the Scriptures.

Engaging Tragedy and Victimhood: the Old Testament

The Old Testament tells of a gracious and just God and of a people called to know and serve him faithfully. When they become victims, they cry out to this God. Central to the Old Testament is the story of God's response to the cry of his people when victims of slavery in Egypt. God calls Moses and through him reveals his name, liberates his people, binds himself to them in covenant, and gives them laws by which to live. In generations following, commemoration of the Passover will become a great annual religious festival. Centuries later, when prophets declare to God's people exiled in Babylon that God will come and set them free, they will speak of this as a new Exodus.

In the Old Testament, God is understood both as rescuing victims and also as vindicating them. God addresses not only the pain of suffering and privation, but also the anguish of injustice; hence the recurring image of God as a righteous judge. For us today, no doubt, the prospect of judgment tends to conjure up the threat of condemnation and punishment. In the Old Testament, however, the opportunity to be heard in court is counted a blessing—it means that injustice will not lie forever hidden or denied with impunity, but will be publicly acknowledged and redressed.

In the OT, God is understood both as rescuing victims and also as vindicating them

Accordingly those who cry out to God cry out not just for their own good but for the vindication of a good God upon whom all human hope and meaning depend. They cry out that God may be glorified.

Victimhood shows its spiritual power to deny God's glory when it tempts his people to either dismiss or be overwhelmed by the demands of faith. Such testing arises both at a personal level (as voiced, for example, in the Psalms) and at a national level (when Israel falls victim to successive foreign empires).

Where in the Old Testament do we see the temptation to *dismiss* victimhood and its demands upon faith? We see it, notably, when the question of suffering (of either the individual or the nation) is too easily answered as God's punishment for sin. This answer reflects a desire to affirm God's control in troubled circumstances and to make sense of these. However, it neither resolves adequately the offence of sin nor expresses adequately God's intended relation to his people. It also dismisses the fact of suffering among the just. It encourages the accusation of innocent victims suffering from disease, handicap or misfortune, thereby reinforcing their experience of victimization. In psalms such as Psalm 69 we repeatedly hear the cry of righteous victims wrongly accused of sin on account of their suffering. Even the prophets themselves are victims of accusation and persecution. For their part, the prophets frame a more faithful answer in terms of forgiveness, a new covenant, a new heart, and new knowledge of a God who is both merciful and just.

The temptation to be *overwhelmed* by victimhood shows itself both in psalms which curse personal enemies and in enraged militancy towards Israel's oppressors. A political Messiah is sought, and God becomes effectively a national patron. A more faithful response is found in the prophetic testimony to God's Suffering Servant.

In the Book of Job we find a sustained exploration of victimhood suffered by a just individual. Although Job is popularly associated today with patience in misfortune, this book is more about his agonized but

Obedience to God takes, for Job, the form of sustained, heartfelt questioning without apparent resolution

faithful response to his victimization. Job faces the temptation, on the one hand, to be *overwhelmed*, despairing of a just God. This temptation is voiced by his wife who invites him to 'Curse God and die.' His friends, on the other hand, urge him falsely to *dismiss* his complaints and admit to deserving what has happened to him. Job resists both temptations. Instead, on the one hand, he faces the grief and injustice of his loss, lamenting in silence for seven days. Lament has an essential place in biblical spirituality. On the other hand he wrestles painfully with God. Obedience to God takes, for Job, the form of sustained, heartfelt questioning without apparent resolution.

The fact of victimhood, then, denies God the liberator and vindicator. Inseparably, its persistence therefore has power to provoke the victim to deny God, evading the demands here of faith. But where faith persists that God wills nevertheless to have the last word, God's name is honoured and the power of victimhood to destroy faith resisted. God's last word would finally be heard, so it was believed, when a Messiah came to fulfil God's purposes on earth with a great cry of welcome: 'Blessed is he who comes in the name of the Lord. Hosanna in the highest!'

Victimhood and the Passion of the Christ

Jesus of Nazareth proclaimed in speech and action the imminent approach of God's kingdom. As he did so, he called people to repentance, restored hope to many victims of disease and social exclusion, and declared the sins of individuals forgiven. In so doing he fulfilled prophecies (as they were seen) of a coming Messiah.

Jesus accepted his Messianic vocation from God. However, his vocation did not match popular expectations of the Messiah as a political leader who would overthrow Roman occupation and restore sovereignty to her victim nation, Israel. Certainly the deeper sovereignty of God which Jesus proclaimed would bring the final vindication of victims. However, this was a sovereignty growing secretly in the midst of the conditions of the world, which conditions included the persistence of victimhood. In the Beatitudes Jesus affirmed the promise of the kingdom to people faithful under various conditions of victimhood. Final liberation and vindication were assured, and the spiritual power of victimhood to defeat faith was even now overcome.

In a radical development, however, the Messiah himself would now take leading place among those who as victims look to God for final liberation and vindication. A catastrophe of cosmic proportions was imminent. The expectation had been that a Messiah would come amidst great welcome to fulfil God's purposes on earth. The rejection and barbaric execution of the Messiah therefore represented the worst scenario imaginable. The crucifixion of any man was seen as an horrific affair, as a spectre threatened by Romans to robbers, insurgents and disobedient slaves. The prospect of the crucifixion of *the Messiah*, of all people, could only be utterly devastating to the human spirit. This was the prospect which confronted Jesus, and which he shared with his disciples. We can hardly overestimate the force of Peter's response: 'Heaven forbid, Lord!'

The prospect of the crucifixion of the Messiah, of all people, could only be utterly devastating to the human spirit

For Jesus himself, the prospect of his execution compellingly tempted him to despair both of God and of humankind. It urged him to despair utterly of God, because if God now allowed his own Messiah to be killed, this would mean that rather than bringing his purposes to final fulfilment God had betrayed and abandoned them in a final way. Jesus has committed himself utterly to the fulfilment of these purposes—but what hope in God could there remain in these circumstances? Accordingly Jesus' death presented itself to him as obscenely futile—as a final, triumphant mockery of the goodness and faithfulness of God. It confronted Jesus with the great final trial or temptation to lose faith and despair utterly of God.

The prospect of his execution also gave Jesus every reason to despair utterly of humankind. Jesus' hope in God involved an implicit hope that God's purposes would be fulfilled among his people. They would be given a new

Jesus' death confronted him with the great final trial or temptation to lose faith and despair utterly of God

covenant, respond faithfully to God, and participate in this fulfilment. Jesus committed himself wholly to awakening such a response among God's people, his hope hinging upon it. Facing his execution, however, such hope for God's people appeared futile. Religious leaders were planning the most outrageous denial of God's good purposes; one of his own disciples would betray him; even Peter who had declared him Messiah would deny knowing him. There had been acts of rebellion, blindness and betrayal among God's people in the past, of course, but there had also been many stories of repentance and renewed faithfulness. This time it was different. If the Messiah himself was rejected by God's people, what hope could now placed in them to be faithful? What possible hope could remain for them?

For Jesus, therefore, the prospect of his crucifixion was a trial of ultimate proportions. It had monstrous power spiritually to compel Jesus to betray God —evading the unfaceable demands of faith either by turning away, or being overwhelmed by it.

Jesus however, met this unqualified trial open in an unqualified way to God. He allowed the unthinkable possibility that even this could be a vocation from God—that against seemingly impossible odds, God's good purposes would yet have the last word. In so doing he shunned evasion in a final way. On the one hand he shunned the temptation of dismissal; in the Garden of Gethsemane he embraced fully the grief of his abandonment by God and by humankind, which intimated the defeat of God's purposes. On the other hand he shunned the inner, personal defeat of faith—he trusted God that his death would yet prove somehow a baptism (Luke 12.50). And in such extremity he continued impossibly to address God with hope, and in so doing address humankind.

If the prospect of the crucifixion of the Messiah presented Jesus with compelling grounds for despair, its execution forever urges the same upon humankind. In Jesus' life we see all goodness and justice, all blessing and promise, coming to fulfilment among us. In his crucifixion we see human beings descend to their worst act, and we 'own' our complicity in this. We have opposed and utterly betrayed God and ourselves. We have renounced the hope and meaning upon which human life depends. Recognition of this now draws us, with Christ, into trial beyond measure. What conceivable hope remains for us, whose only hope lies in the God whom we have utterly rejected and whose purposes we have finally defeated? The temptation is extreme, either to turn away or be overwhelmed.

Jesus Christ, however, now holds our attention. We become attentive to the miracle that, having first accepted this as his vocation, he now refuses either to turn away from or be overwhelmed by what we have done to him. And he addresses us as our victim; he calls us not to turn away from him or from what we have done to him. In so doing he presents us with a darker victim-hood that we have yet encountered, and this at our own hands; but he also demonstrates to us that he is not overwhelmed by it. He does not take the bad into himself as if he 'deserved' it, paralysed by self-pity and resentment, nor does he project the bad on to us, demonizing us with hatred. Rather, in dignity and freedom he addresses God and ourselves: 'Father, forgive them, they do not know what they are doing.'

Thus liberated, we can acknowledge our guilt with dignity endowed by his forgiveness

In so doing, Jesus extends to us his own dignity and freedom. Precisely because his victimhood at our hands has ultimate power to overwhelm us, his forgiveness has ultimate power to set us free, as he is free. Thus liberated, we can acknowledge our guilt with dignity endowed by his forgiveness.

Similarly where we in turn experience victimhood, Christ frees us from its paralysing power. He dispels its ultimate claim upon us. He lifts us beyond its power secretly to make us condemn ourselves in self-hatred and self-pity, or to condemn others in rage and hatred. He bestows upon us his own digni-fied liberty.

The Christian gospel now urges that no victim who comes to see and under-stand Christ will find beyond reach the ultimate promise of vindication. No accomplice in tragic victimization will find beyond reach the ultimate hope of forgiveness. Victims will find, like Jesus, the dignity and grace to forgive. Oppressors will find the humility to confess and ask forgiveness from their victims as from Christ. Jesus carried the dignity of hope—hope for God and for humankind—into the fathomless depths of victimhood.

Jesus is Exalted

Entering into trial beyond measure, Jesus entrusted himself without measure to God. This, he believed, was his inescapable Messianic vocation. Impossibly, his crucifixion would prove the way in which God would fulfil his purposes, revealing Jesus for who he was.

When, in Jesus' resurrection, God reveals him as his son (Romans 1.4), the truth of his passion is simultaneously revealed. The meaning of Jesus' death and resurrection are disclosed together, in relation to each other. It is when we see Jesus' honour that we see his crucifixion as the catastrophe it is for humankind; when we now see Jesus embracing this extremity trusting in God, his honour moves us all the more. But this enhanced honour now deepens in turn the darkness of his victimization—and therefore his embrace of this darkness discloses further still his exalted honour.

In this way the immeasurable force of Jesus' crucifixion as a message of defeat (both for God and for faith in God) and the immeasurable force of his resurrection as a message of victory for these reinforce each other without limit. It is here, in the crucifixion of Jesus, that the command of Satan implicit in every trial—the command to yield to defeat and despair—urges itself with unfathomable power. It is addressed in turn by the resurrection of Jesus with its own unfathomable power.

Questions for Discussion

1 Read the story of Cain and Abel (Genesis 4.1-16). Discuss this in the light of issues of victimhood and evasion, starting with the Lord's rejection of Cain's offering and ending with the Lord's response to Cain's protest that his sentence overwhelms him.

2 The story of Job is about a just man who becomes, ultimately with the permission of God, a victim of Satan—it is Satan who falsely accuses Job of being motivated by self-interest and who asks for license to demonstrate this by testing Job. In the Garden of Eden, who does the serpent falsely accuse, and how? Where else in the Bible might we see Satan at work behind false allegations?

3 *The Zimbabwean* (21-27 Oct '05) published an interview in which Roy Bennett, MP—stripped of his farm and imprisoned for a year—was asked how he spent his time in prison. He said: 'Lock-up in the prisons is at 4pm. So, from then until the lights go out at 8pm, in every cell you hear singing. And its all hymns and religious singing. And you know the voices of the people and how they harmonise—it's unbelievable. It used to make the hair on my arms stand up, it was so beautiful...I would have prisoners coming to me with little slips of paper: "Look up this verse, this chapter," basically pertaining to my situation. It was unbelievable...In prison, I took my hands off the steering wheel and said, "Jesus, you are now in control." Basically, any door that opens up, anything that happens, I go and do it.' Discuss this testimony in relation to 1 Peter 1.1,2.

5

When the Gospel Itself Becomes Captive to Evasion

When we have come to faith in Christ, it may happen that later the gospel loses for us its active power, even though we do not explicitly disavow it.

We may no longer hear it as a message which engages vitally with the demands which victimhood actually makes upon us. We may in practice dismiss or be defeated by these demands without bringing the gospel to bear upon them. We may even conceive the gospel itself in terms captive to the evasion from which it frees us, becoming either dismissive of or overwhelmed by the demands of faith. Thus the church sometimes presents Jesus' resurrection divorced from the darkness of his crucifixion; in so doing it glosses over and *dismisses* the challenge of the cross. Alternatively, the church presents Jesus'

The church sometimes presents Jesus' resurrection divorced from the darkness of his crucifixion

crucifixion without recognizing in it the light of victorious faith, evoking a tragic sense of life as it *overwhelms* our spirit. I illustrate both tendencies below. Both generate spiritualities which rob the gospel of its essence. In truth, the resurrection dawns for us precisely in living contradiction of the darkness of the cross. It opens the horizons of our soul to new life from God precisely as it engages our own deepest darkness.

A Spirituality Captive to Dismissal

The church has seemed sometimes to dismiss tragedy by telling a story with a happy ending in which everything now makes sense, justice is done, reason is upheld and compensation given. It has encouraged too cheap a belief in the gospel which in truth stands always in living engagement with tragic victimhood and with a tragic sense of life.

Consider, for example, some Christian teaching on the victory of Christ. Christ is acclaimed too cheaply today in some praise songs as if a victorious warrior in the spiritual martial arts following a superior performance. However, when early Christians depicted Christ reigning as king from the cross, they knew they asserted a radical contradiction: the only too evident spectre of Jesus' crucifixion as the defeat of God's purposes was in truth a victory. Similarly the church sometimes speaks too casually of Jesus as alive today, and of loved ones as alive with him, in heaven. Geoff Walters has argued that this reflects a Christian accommo-dation, historically, to the Greek doctrine of the immortality of the soul. In truth the hope of resurrection engages grief and lament; it does not allow us to gloss over them, but frees us to enter into them without despairing.

The hope of resurrection does not allow us to gloss over grief and lament, but frees us to enter into them without despairing

Similarly the church sometimes speaks too routinely of Jesus' death as fulfill-ing the divine plan. This was a temptation especially for a medieval church and culture which believed in a timeless, ordered cosmos. But when the risen Lord spoke with his followers walking to Emmaus, he engaged the apparent defeat of God's purposes as revealed in Scripture: this was itself, he urged, according to the Scriptures. Again, the church sometimes presents the cruci-fixion too simply as a moral act of self-privation and self-sacrifice for the good of others. However, Jesus' acceptance of death went beyond this; it required a radical act of trust by Jesus which addresses and contradicts the seeming utter futility of this event.

A Spirituality Captive to Personal Defeat

On other occasions the church has presented the passion of Christ in terms captive to a tragic sense of life—Jesus has been portrayed merely as a pitiful victim. Medieval Christian devotion to Jesus saw him as an object of pity, and this orientation is found still in some Christian spirituality today. It is apparent, indeed, in Mel Gibson's film *The Passion of the Christ* in which the director presents Jesus as an incomprehensible victim; Gibson uses such means as Mary's response to her son's passion to cue tragic sentiment in his audience.

Some other modern spirituality is similarly informed by a tragic sense of life, turning Jesus into a mere icon of victimhood. Good Friday devotions today sometimes come closer to 'lighting a candle for Jesus' than honouring the Christ whose life is the light of humankind. The passion of Jesus here over-whelms with tragic sentiment rather than challenging the power of victimhood to overwhelm. This sentiment is distinctively modern in its link with enraged militancy over victimization.

This militancy has often justified itself theoretically by the Marxist re-interpre-tation of Jewish and Christian hope. It is reflected today in the militant exercise of 'victim power' and in the excesses of 'political correctness.' Sometimes Christ himself gets co-opted by this agenda. In an echo of this, the play *Jesus*

Christ Superstar presents as its real hero the militant Judas, the oppressed one who dares to rail against God for demanding a petulant Jesus' death.

Basically this vision rejects with anger the demands of patient faith. Victimhood can be eliminated; in principle it does not *need* to arise. Such a claim draws encouragement from successive improvements in human well-being through advances in science and technology. In practice, however, this vision can be sustained only at the expense of leaving without hope actual individuals whose victimhood *cannot* presently be eliminated. It also tends to demonize oppressors, fostering a new generation of victims.

Undoubtedly the church has sometimes in the past wrongly suggested that God's will lay in patiently accepting victimhood when it lay instead in greater initiative to eliminate victimhood. However, a vision which denies that victimhood *need* ever arise evades the demands made by victimhood as a present reality, employing a theoretical framework which allows their dismissal. For a clear, succinct treatment of these issues the reader may consult Lesslie Newbigin's article 'The Right to Fullness of Life.'

Embracing Christian Hope Today

In summary, how shall we live with Christian hope today, and witness to this hope among others? Firstly, we need to recognize the temptation posed by victimhood (either our own or that of others) to dismiss victims by one means or another. We need to understand this as a temptation to dismiss the demands of faith in a good and just God and his care for us; to recognize when this temptation presents itself to us, and to our culture; to work with dedication for the liberation and vindication of victims, to the glory of God; and to encourage other people to do the same.

Secondly, it is important to recognize the temptation posed by victimhood to yield to inner personal defeat. We need to understand this as a temptation to yield to the spiritual power of victimhood to overwhelm and paralyse our faith and hope. We need to recognize that such overwhelming is prevalent in our culture today, giving rise to a 'tragic sense of life' and fuelling self-pitying sentiment and rage over victims; to acknowledge the effect of this upon our own spirit; to recognize when this temptation arises for us, and for our culture; to seek to free others from this captivity to the spiritual power of victimhood, restoring hope to their spirits; and to encourage other people to do the same.

Our fundamental calling in all this is to embrace Jesus Christ as the one who has fathomed the ultimate depths of tragedy and victimhood. It is he who, faithful in unqualified trial, can lead us endlessly beyond the evasion of dismissal and personal defeat, so that we overflow with hope (Romans 15.13).

It is he who empowers us to recognize these temptations for what they are, and when they arise for us, to shun them. His victimhood and his vindication by God are *for us*, and sustain us in faith when victimhood brings for us the time of trial.

As we witness to this, let us recognize where the gospel has fallen captive to the evasion it overcomes, and has become complicit either

It is Jesus who can lead us endlessly beyond the evasion of dismissal and personal defeat, so that we overflow with hope

in dismissal of, or personal defeat by, victimhood. Let us also recognize that many people have never grasped how the gospel speaks to their spirit in its trials. In each case let us seek ways of recovering the hope of the gospel in its living engagement with a culture marked by tragic spirituality and victim sensibility.

Questions for Discussion

1 '…the wisest way to cope is not to try to avoid being overwhelmed, and certainly not to expect to be in control of everything; rather it is to live amidst the overwhelmings in a way that lets one of them be the overwhelming that shapes the others' (David Ford, *The Shape of Living*, p xxv) How can we let the gospel overwhelm the varied things which oppress our spirits day by day?

2 'There is a dangerous concern with spiritual technology, with method and technique, the carrying over into the spiritual realm of the corrupting effect of consumer capitalism. So we see spirituality sold as a commodity…' (Ken Leech, *The Sky is Red*, 1997, p 122). Why, in the light of our exploration of victimhood, is the concern Leech describes a distortion of Gospel spirituality?

3 'The poor, the deprived, the handicapped are not primarily a problem to be solved by the rich, the comfortable and the strong. They are the bearers of a witness without which the strong are lost in their own illusions. They are the trustees of a blessing without which Church cannot bless the world.' (Lesslie Newbigin, 1978, p 346. (For full text, see http://www.newbigin.net/searches/detail.cfm?ID=1567) Who, having been a victim, has brought blessing and inspiration to you personally?

More questions for discussion of the issues raised in this booklet can be found on the Grove web site at www.grovebooks.co.uk, together with further quotation references and links to other resources.

6 Bibliography

Some Books and Articles Cited

Rene Girard, *I See Satan Fall Like Lightning* (New York: Orbis, 2001).

Os Guinness, 'More Victimized than Thou,' in Os Guinness and John Seel (eds), *No God But God: Breaking with the Idols of Our Age* (Chicago: Moody Press, 1992).

David Hay and Kate Hunt, *Understanding the Spirituality of People who don't go to Church* (Nottingham: Centre for the Study of Human Relations, University of Nottingham, 2000).

Christopher Lasch, *The Culture of Narcissism* (London and New York: Norton, 1979).

Melvyn Mattews, *Delighting in God* (London: Fount, 1987).

Alistair McFadyen, *Bound to Sin: Abuse, Holocaust and the Christian Doctrine of Sin* (Cambridge: Cambridge University Press, 2000).

Sebastian Moore, *The Crucified Is No Stranger* (London: Darton, Longman and Todd, 1977).

Lesslie Newbigin, 'The Right to Fullness of Life,' in *A Vision for Man: Essays on Faith, Theology and Society*, Samuel Amirtham (ed) (Madras: Christian Literature Society, 1978). The text of this article is available at www.Newbigin.Net.

George Steiner, *The Death of Tragedy* (New York: Oxford University Press, 1961).

Geoff Walters, *Why do Christians find it hard to grieve?* (Carlisle: Paternoster Press, 1997).

Simone Weil, 'The Love of God and Affliction' in Weil, *Waiting on God*, Emma Crauford (trans) (London: Routledge and Kegan Paul, 1951).

Patrick West, *Conspicuous Compassion* (London: Civitas, 2004).